FeARSOME
CReATUReS

Illustrated by Q2A Media and Nicholas Forder
Written by Rona Skene and Simon Smith

PaRragon

Bath · New York · Singapore · Hong Kong · Cologne · Delhi · Melbourne

Designed by Lisa Nutt

First published by Parragon in 2007
Parragon
Queen Street House
4 Queen Street
Bath BA1 1HE, UK

978-1-4054-9468-7

Printed in China

Contents

Awesome Animals 4
Meet the Big Cats 6
The Bear Facts 8
Hot-shot Hunters 10
Deadly Killers 12
Bad-tempered Beasts 14
Amazing Animal Awards 16
The Secret
    World of Snakes 18
Rain Forest Reptiles 20
Champion Killers 22
Fabulous Fangs 24
Deadly Desert Dwellers 26
Shake, Rattle, and Roll 27
Mega Menu 28
Feats and Facts 30
Mini Monsters... the Truth! 32
House of Tiny Terrors 33
Mini Monster Champions 34
Touchy Feely
    Creepy Crawlies 36

Mini Monster Menu 37
Tiny but Deadly 38
For my Next Trick 40
Mini Acting Stars 41
Who Lives Here? 42
Fight! The Fact File 44
Ocean Tough Guys 46
Armed and Dangerous 47
Scary Shark File 48
World's Weirdest Sharks 50
Behave! 51
Ocean Giants 52
Creatures of the Deep 54
Battle of the Reef 56
Daring Defense 58
Watch Out! 60
Lair of the Sea Monster 62
Index and credits 64

AWESOME Animals

Meet some of the planet's most powerful predators, fiercest fighters, and best hunters.

BiGGEST... cat
The Siberian tiger is the largest member of the cat family. It roams in remote parts of Russia and China, but there are only about 400 of these magnificent creatures left.

BiGGEST... bully
The white rhino proves that even vegetarians can be dangerous! They charge at anyone they consider a threat, and male rhinos competing for a female fight ferociously.

BiGGEST... bear
The Kodiak bear, a type of grizzly, is the largest bear in the world. Its favorite food is salmon, which it swipes out of the water with its extra-long, razor-sharp claws.

Now that's BIG!!!!!

BIGGEST... of them all

The African elephant is the world's biggest land animal. Males can grow to 13 feet tall and weigh about 15,400 pounds. That's almost as much as a British double-decker bus!

FACT or FICTION?

A lizard's bite can kill!

FACT!

The gila monster kills birds, mammals, and other lizards with its venomous fangs. This lizard's venom is as strong as a rattlesnake's.

Bats feed on human blood!

FICTION!

Dracula stories give bats a bad name. Only vampire bats drink the blood of other animals—but rarely humans'. Most bats eat only insects.

Alligators have 3,000 teeth!

FICTION!

Alligators have about 80 teeth, but they replace them when they fall out or get worn away. Alligators can go through 3,000 teeth in a lifetime!

Meet the BIG Cats

Big cats make formidable hunters. Their super-sharp senses, stealth, agility, and strength help them to search, stalk, and kill their prey with professional precision.

ROARING SUCCESS
Lions live in family groups headed by the fiercest, most dominant male lion. A male lion's roar is so loud it can be heard up to 5 miles away!

FISHERMAN'S FRIEND
The jaguar waits by the water's edge, attracting fish by batting the surface of the water with its tail. When it spies a fishy treat, the jaguar lashes out, spearing it with its sharp claws.

SPEED MACHINE
Cheetahs are the fastest of the big cats. They can sprint short distances at an incredible 70mph—this would break the speed limit on a highway!

FIERCE FIGHTERS

The Siberian lynx is a fearless predator, often tackling animals three times its size. It will even attack reindeer if it gets the opportunity.

HEAT KEEPER

A snow leopard's large, furry paws act like snowshoes to help it move easily over ice and snow. It can even wrap its tail around its body like a cloak to keep in the heat.

CRAFTY CAT

The caracal uses its large, super-swivelling ears to locate prey. Each ear is controlled by 20 muscles, enabling the caracal to twitch it in all directions.

The BEAR Facts

Most bears avoid trouble, but once they decide to attack, their strength, ferocity, and determination make them un-bear-able.

WANTED...
Scary Polar

APPEARANCE: Thick white or cream-colored fur.

WATCH OUT FOR: Aggression. Polar bears will eat anything they can kill—including humans.

WANTED...
Gruesome Grizzly

APPEARANCE: Long claws, brown fur.

WATCH OUT FOR: Speed. Grizzly bears can run downhill at more than 30mph—which is faster than an Olympic sprinter.

WANTED...
Spectacled Hiker

APPEARANCE: Beige-colored markings across the face and chest.

WATCH OUT FOR: Climbing. Spectacled bears sleep and feed in trees. They're unlikely to attack unless provoked.

WANTED...
Black Attack

APPEARANCE: Brown, cinammon, or even cream-colored fur.

WATCH OUT FOR: Powerful front paws. Black bears will attack humans only if cornered or threatened.

WANTED...
Sun Riser

APPEARANCE: Yellow markings around the muzzle, eyes, and on the chest.

WATCH OUT FOR: Large paws. Sun bears have feet that are turned inward—perfect for climbing up trees.

Killer Creature Joke Store

Ha ha ha ha ha ha!

Ha ha ha Ha!

Why do bears have fur coats? Because they'd look stupid in sweaters!

What's white, furry, and shaped like a tooth? A molar bear!

What do you call a grizzly with no fur? Fred bear!

What kind of bears like to hunt in the rain? Drizzly bears!

What's white, furry, and plays cards? A poker bear!

Hot-shot HUNTERS

Finding a meal is hard work in the wild, and it takes a lot of practice to become a good hunter. Predators hunt their prey in three ways: by stalking, by chasing the prey down, and by attacking in a pack.

Lionesses hunt in groups to catch food for the rest of the pride. Smaller females chase the prey toward the heavier lionesses, who kill the prey.

African golden jackals hunt in pairs, chasing their prey until it is too tired to fight back. Then they deliver a fatal bite in the animal's soft belly.

Servals hunt their prey by sight and sound instead of scent. They often like to play with their catch before eating it.

SAVANNA scavangers

Many animals of the savanna are scavengers—which means they eat dead animals.

Vulgar Vultures

These bald-headed birds have a good sense of smell. They soar above the savanna looking for wounded or dead animals to feast on.

Horrible Hyenas

Hyenas have mighty jaws that can crush large bones as easily as twigs. A hyena's strong stomach can even digest the bones, horns, and teeth of their prey.

African wild dogs are the most successful hunters—they catch their prey 70–90 percent of the time. Sumatran tigers only have a 10 percent success rate.

FIND THE SAVANNA ANIMAL STICKERS AND PUT THEM WHEREVER YOU LIKE IN THIS PICTURE.

DEADLY KILLERS

The search for food is ongoing in the wild. Some clever creatures have found fiendishly inventive ways to catch and eat their live prey.

Leopards can't fly, can they?

MAKE IT SNAPPY

The saltwater crocodile catches land animals by knocking them into the water with its long, powerful tail and gobbling them up whole. Animals too large to be swallowed are first torn into chunks by the croc's teeth.

TREETOP MEAL

The leopard is the best climber of all the big cats. It drags its prey up into a tree to feast in peace, away from the lions and hyenas who might try to steal the meal.

FAST-TRACK FOOD

Like the African golden jackal, the coyote uses its stamina to stalk prey over long distances before pouncing. It uses its sense of smell to track its victim, then attacks when the prey is exhausted.

DANGER MOUTH

A clouded leopard's jaws can open wider than any other cat's, and its teeth are the longest for its size. Its 2-inch-long canine teeth are the same length as a tiger's, even though tigers are 10 times bigger!

P-PICK UP A PENGUIN

The gigantic leopard seal's favorite prey is penguin. It chases and grabs the bird, thrashes it back and forth until its skin strips away, and then pops the peeled penguin in its mouth.

Bad-TEMPERED Beasts

Some animals are more dangerous when they are defending their territory, protecting their young, or avoiding being eaten.

WICKED Wrestler

Black rhinos get very cranky if their territory is invaded and will charge intruders at more than 37mph. A group of rhinos is known as a "crash"—bet you can guess why!

POWERFUL Boxer

Gorillas are peaceful creatures, but a huge male silverback can easily kill a human with a single blow. Before attacking, he will beat his chest and bare his teeth to try to scare the attacker away.

Karate KICKER

Ostriches can't fly away from danger, but they can kill a full-grown lion with a single kick. They can also outrun most pursuers, such as lions, leopards, and hyenas.

Warning: Bad-tempered Beasts!

This cranky crowd of creatures needs lessons in anger management!

← When a hippopotamus is in a bad mood, it can overturn a fishing boat, tossing the sailors into the water and attacking them with its foot-long, lethal tusks.

→ Male warthogs fight each other violently over females. They charge head-on at one another, clashing their heads and goring each other with their short, sharp tusks.

← Never argue with a cape buffalo! This mean-minded mammal can easily defeat a lion silly enough to attack it, and some have even attacked human hunters.

AMAZING Animal Awards

There's a lot more to animals than just being scary. Learn some of the super secrets of the awesome predators that make planet Earth such a wild place.

Rarest Predator

The beautiful white Bengal tiger is very rare—there are only about 150 in the whole world that we know about. Habitat loss and illegal hunting are threats to the species.

Thirstiest Animal

Elephants drink by sucking water through their long trunks. They can slurp up to 50 gallons at a time—that's a whole tubful!

They're all so clever!!

Coolest Camouflage

A panther is a black leopard that has spots, just like a regular leopard. Panthers live in areas with a lot of trees, where their dark color is good camouflage.

Creepiest Creature

Common vampire bats mostly feed on the blood of sleeping mammals. Once bitten, the bat's saliva stops the victim's blood from clotting so that it can lap up the blood.

SCARIEST PREDATOR ALERT

The Nile crocodile is one of the most feared predators on the planet, and also one of the most amazing!

It can grow up to 20 feet long.

Its eyes and nostrils are perched right on top of its head, so that the croc can see and breathe while it hides its huge body underwater.

A mom croc protects her babies from danger by popping them in her mouth. Nobody in their right mind would look in there!

Crocodiles have been around for 200 million years—which makes them older than a T–rex!

In 2005, a croc weighing 2,200 pounds was found in Uganda. It is thought to have eaten 83 people before its capture.

The Secret World of SNAKES

Snakes are amazing reptiles! They first slithered on Earth 140 million years ago, and today there are more than 2,000 different species.

The garter snake, like all snakes, uses its tongue to taste and smell the air around it. Its tongue is forked, so it can taste even more of the air in one flick.

Snakes are cold-blooded, which means that they can't warm themselves up. The banded rock rattlesnake will sunbathe in the sun, then hide in a shady spot to cool down.

TEMPER Tantrums

This bunch of reptilian rascals are the ones that most often attack humans. They might not be the most poisonous, but they are definitely the most bad-tempered!

Rattlesnake

Indian cobra

Vipers, such as the gaboon viper, have super-flexible jaws that can disconnect and open amazingly wide to swallow prey much bigger than themselves.

A python kills by winding its body around prey and squeezing REALLY tight until the creature dies. A rock python was once found with a whole leopard in its stomach!

Some snakes bite their prey, injecting fatal venom through their ferocious fangs. Snakes are immune to their own poison, so it doesn't matter if one accidentally bites its own tongue!

Saw-scaled viper

Puff adder

YIKES! GET ME OUTTA HERE!

RAIN FOREST Reptiles

The rain forest is full of tasty creatures—the ideal hunting ground for the snakes that patrol the forest floor and lie in wait in the trees.

FIND THE RAIN FOREST SNAKES STICKERS AND PUT THEM ANYWHERE IN THIS PICTURE.

The boa constrictor lies in wait before it grabs its victim. It wraps itself around the creature and squeezes really hard, suffocating it.

Some snakes spend their lives in trees. The green cat snake is perfectly camouflaged for a life among the leaves.

True or False?

Snakes can swim.

TRUE The Anaconda is the champion in the water. When it spies some tasty prey, it wraps itself around the animal and holds it underwater until it drowns.

Snakes change color.

TRUE Few snakes are known to have this ability. However, a new species of snake, called the Kapuas mud snake, has been found to change color spontaneously.

All snakes lay eggs.

FALSE Some snakes, such as the green mamba, give birth to live babies. A newly hatched green mamba is just as poisonous as its parents!

RECORD BREAKER

The reticulated python holds the record for the world's longest snake at 33 feet. That's almost as long as a bus!

The emerald boa lives in dense forest. Its fantastic heat-seeking sensors allow it to hunt for prey in total darkness.

The bright green boomslang is a deadly tree dweller. The venom in its grooved rear fangs makes victims bleed to death internally.

Champion KILLERS

Some snakes kill using spectacular strength and power. Some rely on their super-sharp senses to defeat their victims. Others deliver fatal venom. All of them are formidable predators!

COBRA

Location: Tropical and desert regions (Asia and Africa).

Top skills: Spitting, paralyzing.

Main prey: Cobra venom works gradually by paralyzing the victim. At first, the creature stops moving, then its heart stops and the creature dies.

PIT VIPER

Location: Southeast Asia and The Americas.

Top skills: Sharp senses, striking.

Main prey: The pit viper has a heat-sensitive spot between its eyes. It uses this to locate live creatures with deadly accuracy.

I'M S-S-SCARED!

WATER MOCCASIN

Location: Southeastern United States.

Top skills: Teasing, poisoning.

Main prey: The young cottonmouth has a yellow tip on its tail. It waves this about to lure prey closer, so it can strike with its poisonous fangs.

RAT SNAKE

Location: North America.

Top skills: Squeezing, climbing.

Main prey: The rat snake kills rodents by squeezing them to death. If it can't wrap itself around the prey, it pushes the poor rat against a rock and squashes it.

SEA KRAIT

Location: Tropical seas.

Top skills: Swimming, striking.

Main prey: The sea krait swims at night, relying mostly on scent to find its prey. It grasps its victim then holds on tight until its venom has paralyzed its prey.

DEATH ADDER

Location: Australia, New Guinea.

Top skills: Teasing, accuracy.

Main prey: The death adder rarely misses its prey and it never wastes its venom. A death adder has only 85 milligrams of venom and it strikes its prey fast!

Fabulous FANGS

Some snakes have special, pointed teeth called fangs. These inject poison into the snakes' victims, paralyzing their prey or killing them instantly.

The Indian cobra, like all venomous snakes, has fangs that are joined to bags of poison in its head. When the snake bites down, the poison flows from the bags to the fangs and into the victim.

Vipers have mega-long fangs that would get in the way—so they fold up in the roof of the snake's mouth when they're not needed. Very tidy!

Ha ha ha ha ha ha!

Silly Snake Joke Store

What do snakes do after a fight? They hiss and make up!

What does a snake wear to a party? A boa tie!

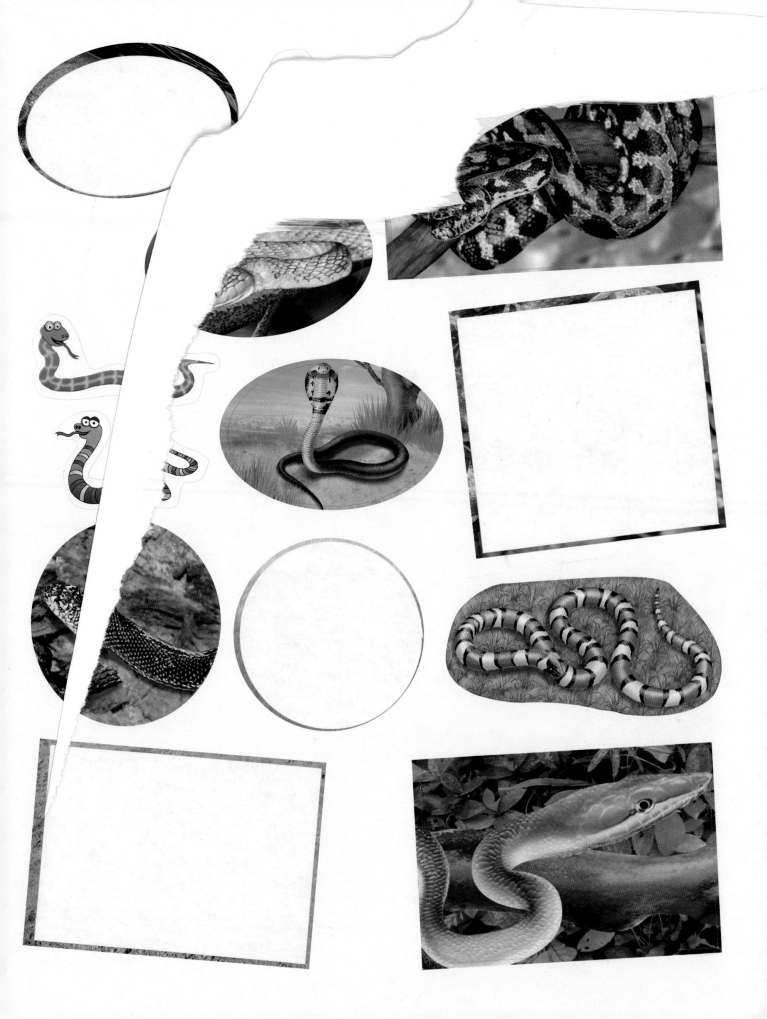

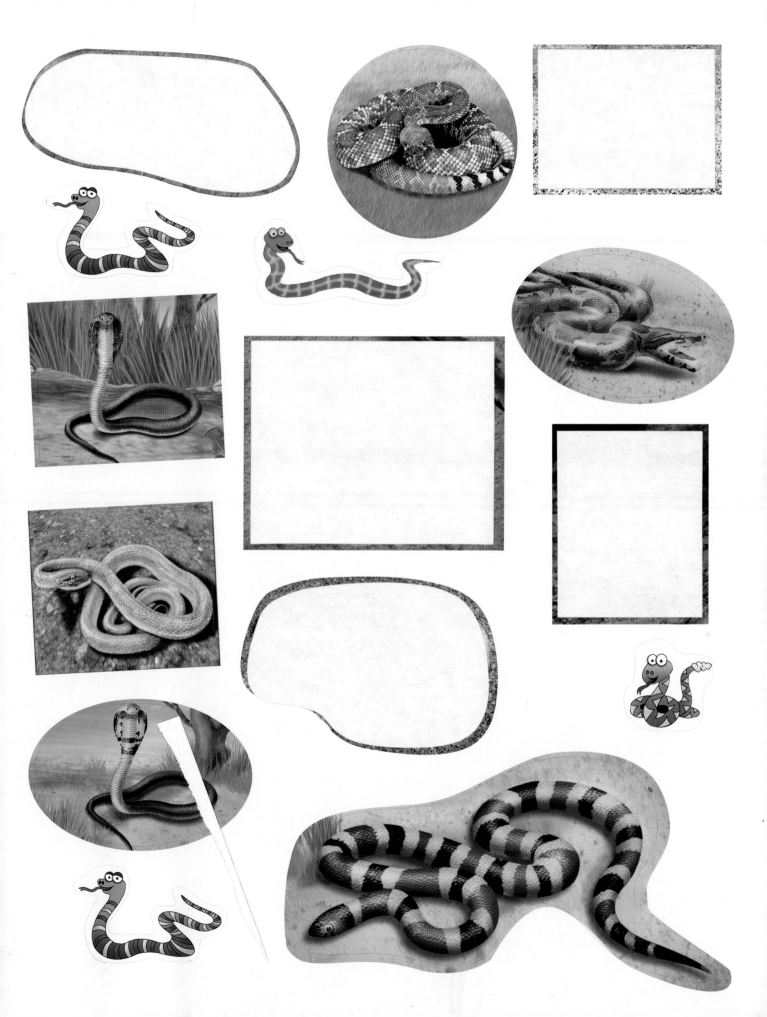

Some snakes, such as the mangrove snake, have short, sharp front fangs. They hold onto their prey after biting, then "chew" to get venom into the prey.

Like some other snakes, the vine snake has poisonous fangs at the back of its mouth. First it bites, then it shuffles the victim to the back of its mouth to deliver the fatal dose of venom.

The beautiful coral snake is highly venomous but, luckily for most humans, its tiny mouth and fangs make it difficult for it to bite people.

Why did the boa constrictors get married? Because they had a crush on each other!

What is a snake's favorite subject? Hisssssssstory!

What kind of snake can do math in the dark? A night adder.

Deadly DESERT Dwellers

Many snakes adapt themselves in clever ways to the dry and harsh conditions of the desert.

FIND THE DEADLY DESERT SNAKE STICKERS AND PUT THEM ANYWHERE IN THIS PICTURE.

The Egyptian cobra, like all cobras, has a flap of skin on its neck that it puffs out when it is angry.

Sidewinders move sideways across sand so that only two small parts of their body touch the sand at a time.

The horned viper has horny scales over its eyes to protect them from the glare of the desert sun.

SHAKE, RATTLE, and ROLL

The fascinating rattlesnake lives in the deserts of North America. Its venom is deadly, but it usually prefers to slither away from humans than stay and bite!

WRIGGLY WARNING

Rattlesnakes, such as the western diamond rattlesnake, warn off their enemies with a menacing rattling sound, made by shaking interlocking rings of hard scales on the end of their tails.

POTENT POISON

The Mojave rattlesnake can easily be mistaken for a diamondback. But the Mojave has a very potent venom, making it one of the most dangerous rattlesnakes in the United States.

CUNNING CAMOUFLAGE

Pacific rattlers blend perfectly into their sandy surroundings and patiently wait for an unsuspecting desert creature to pounce on!

MEGA Menu

What do snakes eat? Anything and everything living! If a creature crawls, buzzes, runs, slithers, or flies, you can be sure there's a hungry snake somewhere, ready to gobble it up!

YUMMY APPETIZERS

A CHEWY LITTLE MORSEL →
The brown snake's favorite snack is snails. It wedges the snail between the ground and a rock, then pulls the fleshy snail out with its specially adapted teeth.

← ANT NEST SOUP
Blind snakes break into ants' nests and suck up huge mouthfuls of ants. A mouthful of ants must be terrifically tickly!

WHICH ONE DID THEY SAY LIKED SNAKES?

MIGHTY MAINS

EGGS-ELLENT MEAL →
An African egg-eating snake can stretch its mouth to three times the size of its head to swallow an egg whole.

← BIG MEAT FEAST
The rock python is the biggest snake in Africa. It is an exceptionally fierce predator, and will swallow whole goats, small antelope, and even crocodiles!

DELIGHTFUL DESSERTS

MUD PIE, TOAD STYLE →
The hognose digs tasty toads out of their burrows with its spade-shaped snout.

← ICING ON THE CAKE
A coral snake's idea of food heaven is a smaller snake, like this crowned snake.

FEATS and FACTS

Snakes come in all shapes and sizes—they can be as small as a worm, as heavy as a sumo wrestler, or as long as a bus. Read some of the best freaky facts here.

THE SNAKE AWARDS

MARVELOUS MOTHER
The king cobra is the only snake in the world that builds a nest on the ground for its babies. It lays 20–30 eggs and guards them until the baby snakes are born.

HEAVYWEIGHT CHAMP
The anaconda is the heaviest snake on Earth. It can weigh as much as 500 pounds or 2.5 dads! Its body can be 12 inches around—fatter than a basketball.

RECORD RACER
The black mamba is one of the speediest snakes on Earth. It can move at up to 12mph—as fast as a human can run—to catch lizards, birds, and rats.

SUPER SWIMMER
All snakes are pretty good swimmers, but sea snakes flatten their tails to push them extra speedily through the water. They can swim for up to two hours underwater.

DID YOU KNOW?

Like all snakes, the garter snake doesn't have ears on the outside of its body, but it still has fantastic hearing—it can pick up the tiniest sounds and vibrations through its skin.

place sticker here

Australia has more venomous snakes than any country—9 out of the 10 most poisonous snakes live there, such as this Australian copperhead!

A milk snake, like all snakes, sheds its skin. When this happens, the scales over its eyes become cloudy and it can't see very well, so it hides away until it can see again.

Mini Monsters... the Truth!

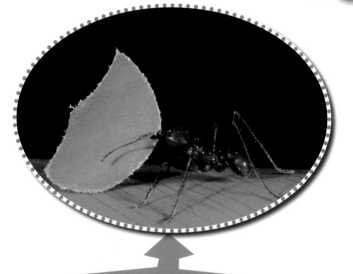

This ant has six legs and three body sections.

Mini monsters are all around you... right now! Planet Earth is full of millions of tiny creepy-crawly creatures.

Insects are the most common mini monsters. They are made different from us. They have six legs, their bodies are made up of three sections, and their skeleton is on the outside of their body. Imagine if your bones were on the outside and you had to run using six legs!

Insects have antennae to feel, hear, and taste the things around them.

The long-horned beetle's antennae are as long as the rest of its body!

Some insects have wings for flying toward food or escaping from danger. Butterflies are insects with very beautiful wings. Some of them have eye patterns on their wings to trick their enemies into thinking they are big fierce creatures.

A butterfly with fake eyes on its wings.

Yuck yuck yuck yuck!

House of Tiny Terrors

You don't have to go
very far to meet amazing mini monsters.
There are plenty sharing your home, your
garden, and even your body!

← Silverfish are slithery flat insects that live in dark, damp corners. They eat food scraps, sugar, fabrics, and even glue!

→ Spiders qualify as mini monsters because they have fangs for biting their prey. However, they are arachnids, not insects. They have eight legs and their bodies are made up of two parts, not three.

← Head lice are tiny, brown wingless creatures that are perfectly suited for living in a human's hair. Their strong pincers help them hold on tight. They live off blood... Yuck!

→ Bumblebees are the most peace-loving of all bees. They never attack in swarms, and some types of bumblebee can't even sting.

Mini Monster Champions

It's not easy being tiny. Mini monsters have to develop superpowers of strength or cunning just to survive. If these creatures were human, they'd be world champions!

Caterpillars are incredibly fast growers. It's possible for a newborn caterpillar to grow a thousand times bigger in just a few days.

The **GROWTH** award goes to...

The **STRENGTH** award goes to...

The rhinoceros beetle can lift things 850 times heavier than itself. If you were that strong, you'd be able to lift up a bus.

A Borneo stick insect is the world's longest insect at more than 14 inches. Measure your arm, and see how it compares.

Mini monster Joke Store

Ha ha ha ha ha ha!

How do bees brush their hair? With a honey comb!

How do bees get to school? On the school buzz!

The **SMELL** award goes to...

A female emperor moth makes a tiny amount of scent that a male emperor moth, with its super senses, can sniff out over half a mile away.

The first **HIGH JUMPING** award goes to...

The **LENGTH** award goes to...

The froghopper is the highest insect jumper. It can clear 28 inches. As it jumps it accelerates faster than a space shuttle!

The second **HIGH JUMPING** award goes to...

A flea can jump about 150 times its own height. If you could do that, you would be able to jump over a building.

What do ants take when they are sick? Ant-ibiotics!

What do bees wear on the beach? Bee-kinis!

Ha ha ha ha ha ha!

What are caterpillars scared of? Dog-erpillars!

Touchy Feely
Creepy Crawlies

Mini monsters use their fantastic senses to hunt, to escape, and to find themselves a mate.

Talk to the Knees

A field cricket listens with its knees. It has tiny ears on its front legs. Imagine if you had to stick your knees in the air to hear!

Eye Spy

Spiders have supersensitive hairs on their bodies that detect the slightest movements. That's very handy when a tasty fly wanders into range.

Hairy Legs

Flies have a lot of eyes—two huge compound eyes that are made up of hundreds of tiny lenses, and three small eyes between the large ones.

Mini Monster Menu

Eating is all-important to mini monsters. They are on a never-ending mission to find enough food.

→ Dung Pie

To a dung beetle, heaven is a lovely, big ball of dung. The beetle rolls a large ball of other animals' dung into its nest. When the baby beetles hatch, they eat the dung.

Munchy Mice

The centipede is a fierce predator with a vicious bite and venomous fangs. Giant centipedes can grow up to 8 inches long and eat mice, frogs, and even snakes.

← Flower Juice

Butterflies suck up their food of flower nectar with a proboscis—a long tube like a straw. When they don't need it, it is coiled up and tucked away.

Grassy Fast Food

Locusts have a huge appetite for plants. A locust eats its own weight in food every day. A swarm of locusts can munch through many fields of crops.

→ Greenfly Snacks

The ladybug is useful to have around because it loves to eat pesky aphids, such as greenfly. Just one ladybug will chomp its way though 5,000 aphids in its lifetime.

Tiny but Deadly

Many mini monsters are expert killers, with a lot of FIENDISH ways to defeat their enemies. Imagine if you were tiny and had to meet one of these in battle!

> If only you could fly!

TARANTULA

Location: South America.
Top skills: Leaping, poison bite.
Main prey: Insects. A tarantula leaps onto its victim and sinks in its hollow fangs, which pump in deadly venom. The prey's insides turn to liquid, which the tarantula sucks up like milk shake.

RED WOOD ANT

Location: Worldwide.
Top skills: Spraying acid.
Main prey: Caterpillars, flies, and other insects. The red wood ant is a fierce hunter. If it is threatened, it sprays out acid powerful enough to eat through an enemy's skin.

> Help me, someone!

PRAYING MANTIS

Location: Tropical countries.
Top skills: Speedy attacks.
Main prey: Insects and lizards.
The praying mantis catches prey with its forelegs, which are armed with fearsome hooks and spines.

DIVING BEETLE

Location: Worldwide.
Top skills: Diving attacks.
Main prey: Water insects and even small fish. This beetle is a great swimmer and can tear apart its prey underwater, using its powerful jaws.

FEMALE MOSQUITO

Location: Worldwide.
Top skills: Sucking blood.
Main prey: Female sucks blood of mammals; male drinks plant nectar. In hot countries, female mosquitoes can pass on deadly diseases, such as malaria, to humans.

BACKSWIMMER

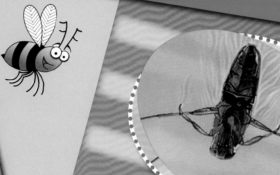

Location: Widespread.
Top skills: Swimming, pouncing.
Main prey: Tadpoles, insects.
The backswimmer swims upside down across ponds and lakes, using its long back legs to row and to pounce on its prey.

For my Next TRICK

Mini monsters use all kinds of fantastic disguises to avoid danger from hungry enemies, or to sneak up on their own prey.

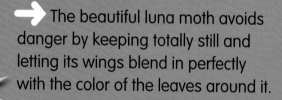

← The flat bark bug disguises itself perfectly as a scrap of tree bark when it wants to avoid unwanted attention.

→ The beautiful luna moth avoids danger by keeping totally still and letting its wings blend in perfectly with the color of the leaves around it.

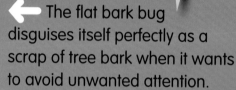

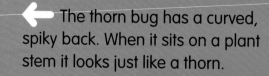

← The thorn bug has a curved, spiky back. When it sits on a plant stem it looks just like a thorn.

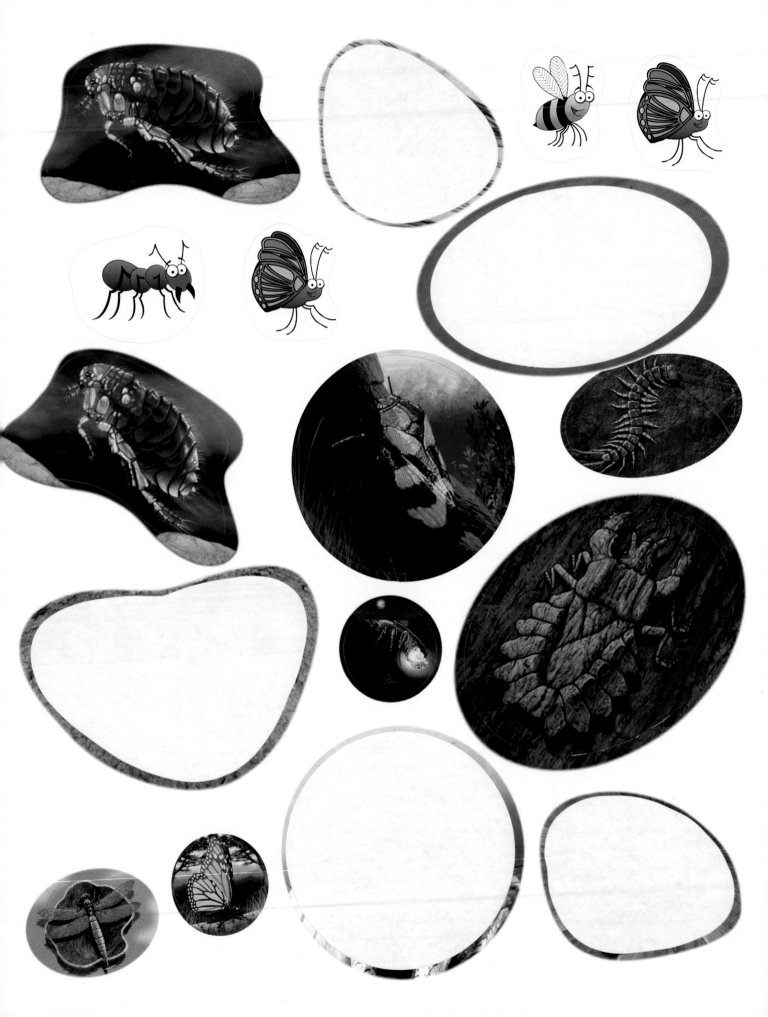

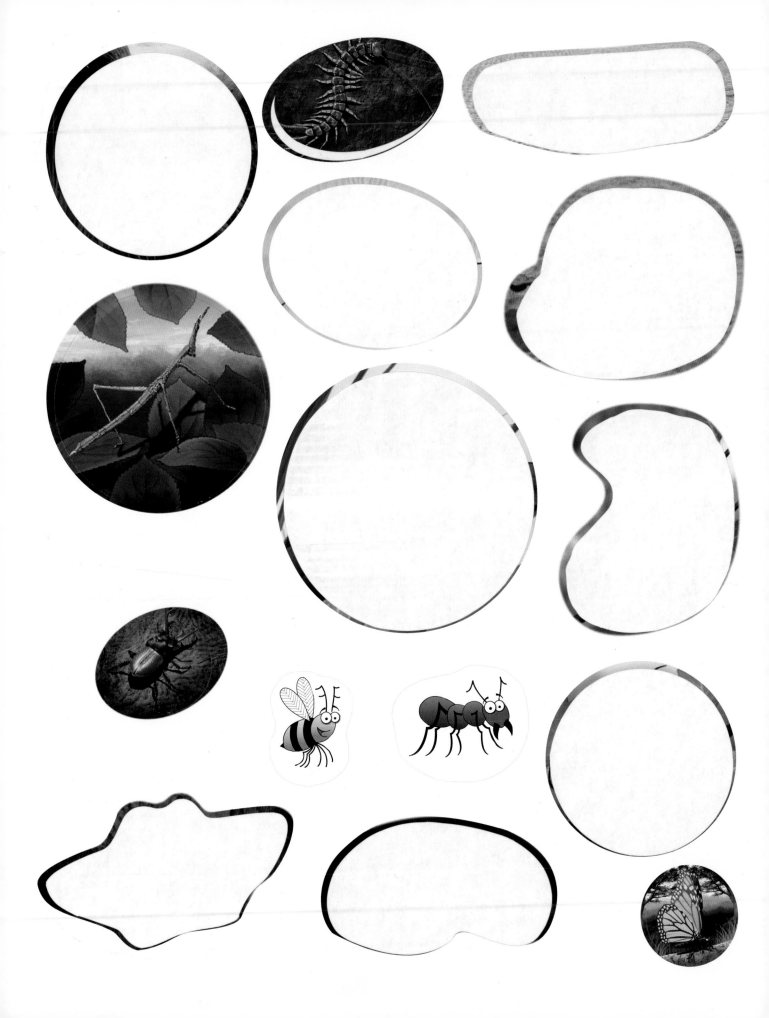

Mini Acting STARS

These insect actors should all get awards
for their crafty performances!
And the winners are...

The death's head hawk moth caterpillar waves its tail when it's in danger. The tail looks like the head of a nasty snake.

The harmless hoverfly defends itself by pretending to be a wasp—hoping that its yellow and black body will fool its enemies.

The flower mantis pretends to be a pretty, pollen-filled flower to attract thirsty insects that it wants to eat.

The eye hawk moth caterpillar looks amazingly like the leaf on which it perches. Can you tell which is the leaf and which is the clever little caterpillar?

Bravo! Bravo!

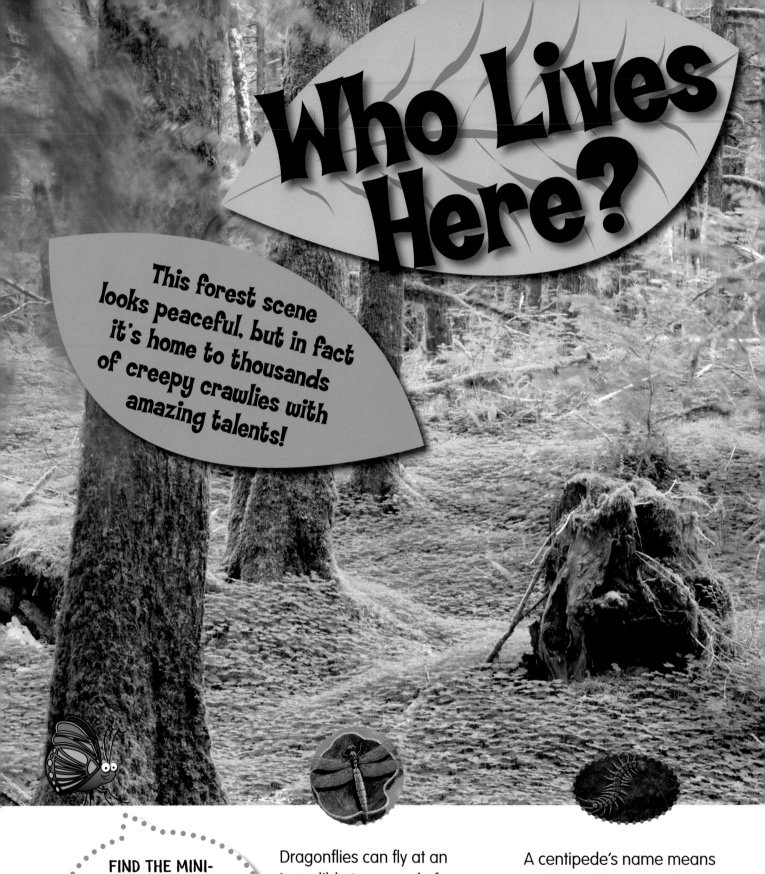

Who Lives Here?

This forest scene looks peaceful, but in fact it's home to thousands of creepy crawlies with amazing talents!

FIND THE MINI-MONSTER STICKERS YOU NEED AND PUT THEM WHERE YOU WANT IN THE FOREST.

Dragonflies can fly at an incredible top speed of 30mph. They can stop in midair, fly backward, and even sideways!

A centipede's name means "100 legs," but some have up to 200. Centipedes also have a pair of poisonous claws to catch prey.

Monarch butterflies travel 2,000 miles from Canada to Mexico in the fall. Then they fly all the way back again in the spring.

A male firefly can make his body glow on and off. If a female likes the way he glows, she attracts him by doing some flashing herself.

Male stag beetles have huge jaws that look like deer antlers. They use them to fight with other stag beetles to win a female mate.

Fight!
The Fact File

These mini monsters have great defending skills. Their enemies may be tough but they have a fight on their hands.

Ants will defend their nests against invaders. This Australian bull ant grabs attackers with its powerful jaws and injects them with poisonous venom.

Some soldier termites have a special elongated snout. When they fight they use it like a paintbrush to smear venom on their enemies.

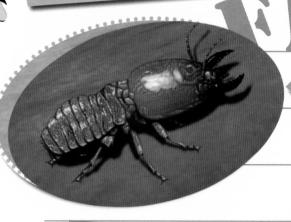

A European devil's coach horse beetle has a secret weapon against attackers—it squirts a jet of fluid from its abdomen (stomach) that smells really disgusting.

FACT
FACT

The brightly colored blister beetle oozes a nasty chemical that irritates anything it touches. It can even make human skin burn and blister.

African killer bees are more bad-tempered than ordinary bees. If they get upset, they gather in huge swarms and can chase an enemy for miles.

The bombardier beetle fights attackers by aiming a fatal jet of boiling-hot chemicals at them. It cooks up the menacing mixture inside its body.

Munch. Yum, yum!

BATTLE of the REEF

A beautiful coral reef looks peaceful, but take a closer look and you'll find a battleground between fierce predators and their prey.

FIND THESE REEF STICKERS AND PUT THEM WHERE YOU WANT ON THE REEF.

Humans love dolphins, but fish aren't so keen on them! Dolphins are expert hunters. They send out powerful sound waves to stun their prey in the water.

The zebra moray eel's favorite food is crab. It skulks in dark crevices, strikes out with its powerful jaws, and grinds the crab with its special flattened teeth.

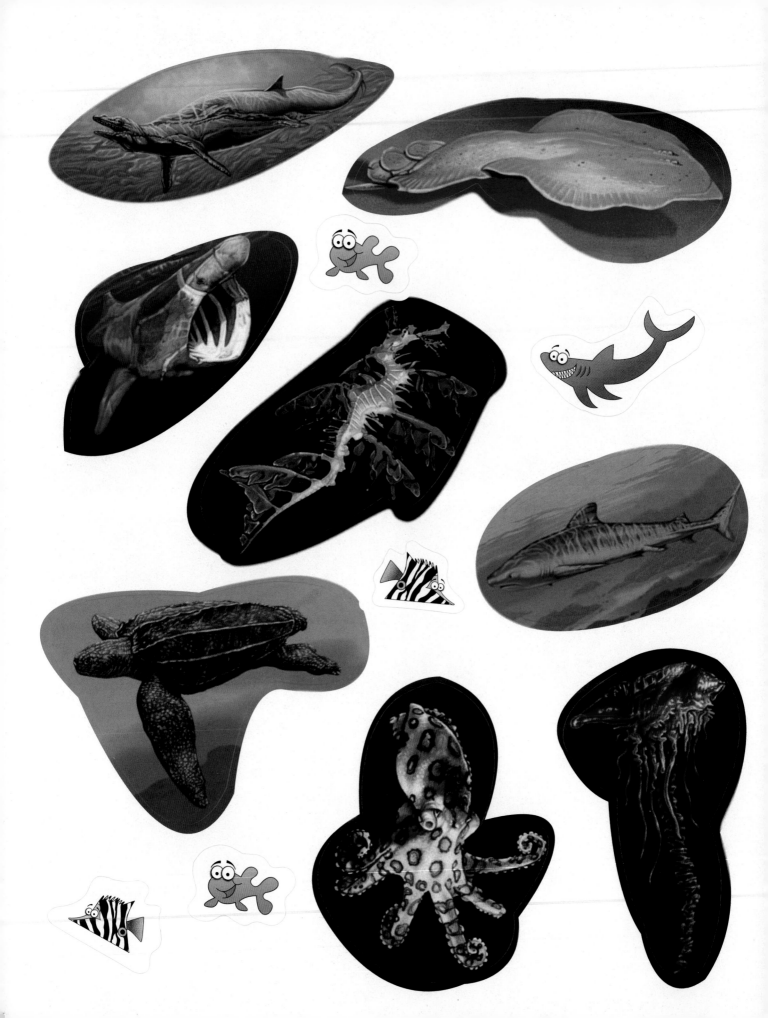

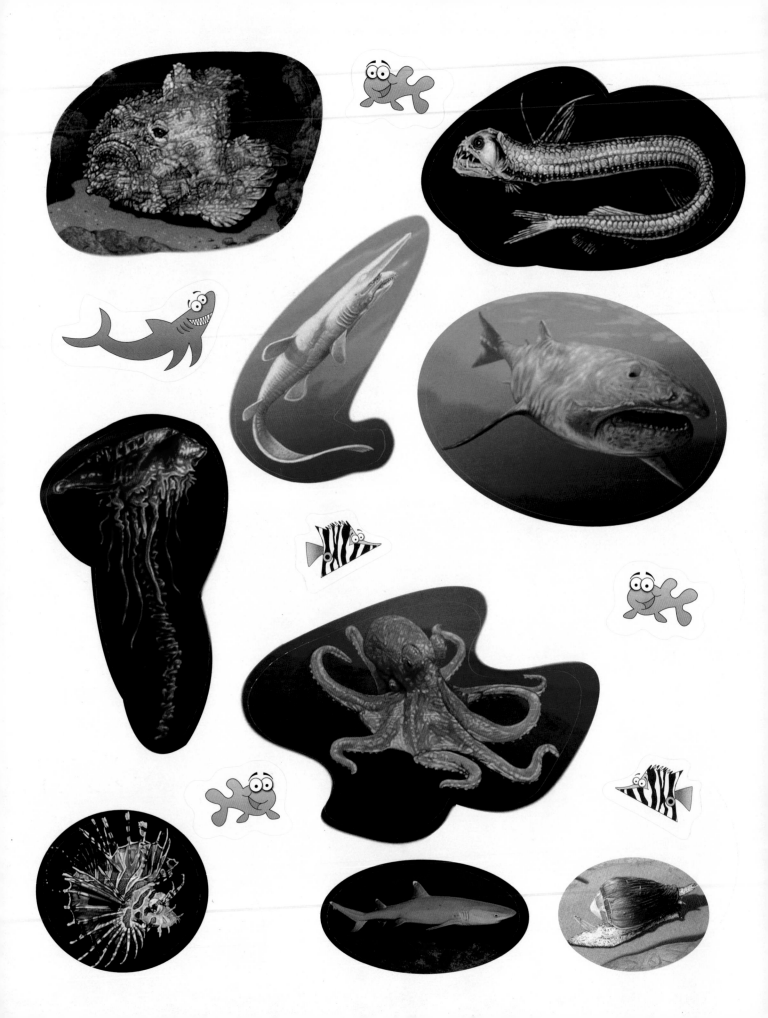

The beautiful feathery fins of the lionfish hide wicked weapons—an array of lethal, poison-tipped spines to put off peckish predators and nosy humans!

White-tipped reef sharks have long, slender bodies and extra-tough skin so that they can wriggle and scrape through gaps in the coral when they chase prey.

When the cone snail spots a tasty passing fish, it fires out a poisoned harpoon attached to its mouth, spearing the fish and paralyzing it.

Watch Out!

Use the spare stickers to create exciting scenes on these real-life pictures of the African Savanna and the rain forest.

Lair of the Sea Monster

Use the spare stickers to create an amazing ocean scene around this real-life picture of a sea wreck.